LET'S VISIT NORWAY

Let's visit
NORWAY

DAVID GASCOYNE

BURKE

ACKNOWLEDGEMENTS

The author and publishers are grateful to the following organisations and individuals for permission to reproduce copyright illustrations in this book:

Keystone Press Agency Ltd.; William Houghton; Eugenie Peter; Patricia Slavik of the Royal Norwegian Embassy.

ISBN 0 222 00302 2 Hardbound
ISBN 0 222 00300 6 Library

Burke Publishing Company Limited
14 John Street, London WC1N 2EJ.
Burke Publishing (Canada) Limited
P.O. Box 48, Toronto-Dominion Centre
Toronto 111, Ontario.

Filmset by Ramsay Typesetting Limited, London and Crawley.
Printed and bound by Holmes, McDougall, Edinburgh.

Contents

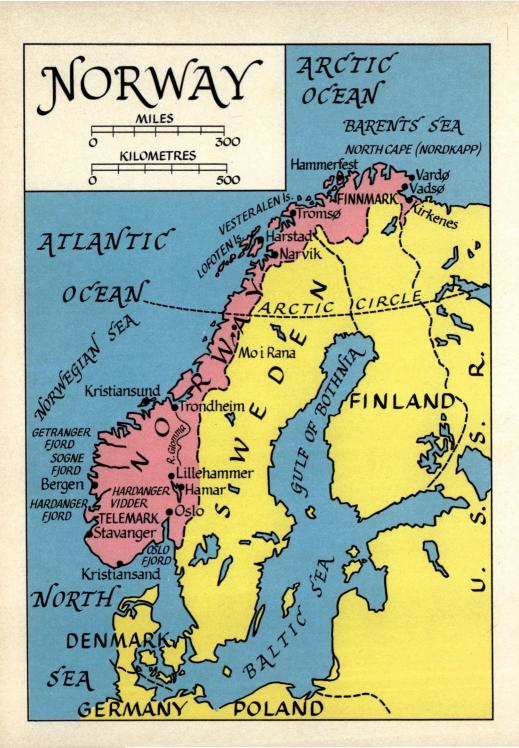

The Country

Norway, or *Norge*, as the Norwegians call their country, has a beauty which is not found in any other European country. Huge towering mountain ranges and narrow valleys, dark pine forests, fast-flowing rivers, superb fjords and lonely bird-inhabited islands all go to make up the scenery of this country. In every sense it is a land of striking contrasts: startling beauty and awesome grimness.

Lille Norge (or "Little Norway") has a population of less than three and a half million people. Unlike Great Britain, for instance, it has no large cities or industrial centres. The capital, Oslo, and the second city, Bergen, have rather less than 600,000 people between them. The towns are even smaller. No town in Norway has more than 60,000 inhabitants.

The name *Lille Norge* is rather misleading, however, for in the physical sense Norway is certainly not small. It is a very long country, narrow in the middle, broadening out again in the south and north-east. From north to south it measures over one thousand miles (1,752 kilometres) and its greatest width is

Water, mountains, wooden houses and fishing boats—the essential ingredients of the Norwegian countryside

270 miles (about 430 kilometres). The total land area, 125,000 square miles (323,750 square kilometres), is rather more than that of the British Isles. The coastline, including the numerous islands, inlets and fjords, is as long as the coastline of Africa or equal to half the circumference of the globe at the Equator.

Norway is bounded to the east by Sweden, Finland and Russia; to the south, west and north by the sea. To the south is the Skagerak (an inlet of the North Sea); to the west the North Sea and the Norwegian Sea, and to the north the Barents Sea.

Norway is the most northerly country in Europe. The extreme south of the country is on the same latitude as the extreme north of Scotland and Alaska. However, due to the Gulf Stream, the climate is much milder than in any other country so far north.

Norway also controls a group of islands in the Arctic Ocean. The name of *Svalbard* (or "Cool Coast") has been given to this dependency. The most important islands are those in the Spitzbergen group.

The first sight of Norway can be rather frightening. Crossing the North Sea from Newcastle to Bergen, the visitor faces a dark and forbidding wall of rock which rises out of the churning waters ahead, topped by a snow-covered mountain peak.

Nearly three quarters of Norway is covered by mountains. A great chain known as the *Kjølen* (or "Keel") stretches from north to south along the frontier with Sweden. The wildest mountains are the *Jotunheimen* (or "Home of Giants"). This range, the biggest in Northern Europe, is in the west of the

Norway is famous for her mountains and glaciers. This glacier is typical. It lies in the mountains between Oslo and Bergen

country, roughly half-way between the coastal towns of Bergen and Trondheim. The *Jotunheimen* have over two hundred peaks over six hundred feet (183 metres) high, as well as many steep valleys and narrow passes. Here is found the *Jostedalsbreen*, the largest icefield in Europe. The Jostedal glacier is nearly seventy-five miles (121 kilometres) long, over one thousand feet (304 metres) deep, and in places as much as seven miles (eleven kilometres) wide.

And everywhere there are lakes. In the mountain areas, the water, reflecting the blue skies, provides a brilliant splash of colour in late summer amid the red, purple and gold of the heather, and of the cranberry and bilberry bushes with which the ground is covered.

Occasionally there is an area of rich farming land between the mountains and the sea; but more often the rock face falls steeply into the waters below. The coastline of Norway is one of the most broken in the world with deep water close inshore. As a result there are a great many good harbours and islands which provide welcome shelter for coastal shipping during fierce Atlantic storms.

In the south the mountains flatten out to form a series of huge, treeless, almost uninhabited plateaus called the *vidder*. For over eight months of the year this part is covered with deep snow. It is broken and cracked by hundreds of narrow inlets through which the sea runs far inland. These deep fissures, which are known as *fjords*, were formed over a million years ago in the Ice Age. The fjords have almost vertical walls of

The countryside near Bergen—its snow-capped mountains and blue water are good reason for Norway's busy tourist industry

rock and are very deep in places. Dotted here and there are small red-painted farms or white villages perched on the steep slopes. There is an offshore fringe of 150,000 rocky islets, of which about 2,000 are inhabited. Two of the most important groups are the Lofoten and the Vesterålen off the north-west coast. Many of the people living along the west coast are either farmers or fishermen. Thousands of them set sail to Lofoten in their small fishing-smacks for the cod-fishing season in February and March of each year. The Lofotens are famous for the huge colonies of birds which breed in the cliff walls. The islands contain many species of sea-birds: puffins, guillemots, kittiwakes, cormorants, black-backed gulls, petrels and the rare sea eagle.

From the jagged mountain creeks or *viks* the fierce Viking pirates once set forth to conquer and plunder new lands. Much. of present-day knowledge of Viking life is obtained from the sagas—heroic stories written by ancient Icelandic writers of Norwegian origin. Many of the sagas tell of the legends of Thor and Odin and other gods of northern mythology; some tell of the gallant deeds of Viking heroes. From the earliest times the Norsemen had been skilful and courageous seamen, venturing far afield in every type of vessel. The Vikings explored Svalbard (Spitsbergen), the White Sea, across the North Sea to Scotland and Ireland, to Normandy, and further afield to Iceland and Greenland, from where Leiv Erikson set out in about A.D. 1000 and came to America, which he called Vinland, because of the vines which grew wild in the eastern coastal area where he landed.

To the north, east and south, a number of fertile valleys find their way deep into the *vidder*. Tree trunks cut on the slopes are floated down the rivers to the wood and paper factories. On the green floors of the valleys are many farms; these are much bigger than those found on the rocky shoulders of the fjords.

Further east, between Oslo (the capital) and Trondheim (Norway's third largest city), the hills and valleys become more gentle and the fields broader. This is the richest and most densely populated area of Norway. South-west from Oslo the

The River Nid running through Trondheim

coast is low but protected by a necklace of islands. This is Norway's favourite holiday region—a region of little towns and villages, with steep narrow streets and gaily painted wooden houses set in garden plots bright with flowers.

From Trondheim, northwards, the country becomes steadily more wild and desolate. The Arctic Circle cuts across central Norway. North of it begins the land of the Midnight Sun. There, for two or three months in the summer, the sun never rises. The Circle is in some ways a natural frontier.

Troms and Finnmark, the northern counties of Norway, would be totally covered with ice and snow if it were not for the existence of the Gulf Stream. This is an ocean current which brings warm water from the Gulf of Mexico right up to the

A herd of reindeer

Atlantic; the sea never freezes as a result. Hammerfest in Finnmark, the northern-most town in the world, is often warmer than Oslo.

All round this barren-looking coast to the Russian frontier, near the town of Kirkenes, there are numerous farms and fishing settlements tucked away in corners sheltered from the harsh climate. The inland plateau of Finnmark, where Norway broadens out again, does not benefit much from the Gulf Stream; here the wandering Lapps with their herds of reindeer manage to make a modest living among inhospitable wastes.

14

The Gulf Stream regulates the climate of Norway. It brings rain and warmth from the south-west, so the west coast is mild in temperature and rainy; the grass is rich and lush; and plum, apple and other trees grow readily in the fertile soil. In the east, however, it is much colder and drier; the forests consist mainly of fir and dwarf birch.

Climate is of very great importance to Norway. In the past it often meant the difference between life and death for the farmer and fisherman. Winter storms at sea or a bad harvest were disasters; entire families starved without enough food to last them throughout the winter months. Happily, this

Traditionally designed trim wooden houses are sometimes painted white or yellow like these

uncertainty is in the past with the advent of modern techniques but climate still plays a major part in the livelihoods of the majority of Norwegians.

Whatever his trade or profession the true Norwegian never feels very far from the land or the sea. The doctor and politician, the professor and factory worker, the banker and teacher, all have fathers or grandfathers, uncles, aunts or cousins working on the land or harvesting the seas for fish. A great many town-dwellers have fond memories of trim wooden houses, fishing-boats on lakes or fjords, and stony fields which their ancestors had cultivated on the bleak mountainsides.

A century ago town life barely existed in Norway. Oslo, the capital, is often called "the largest village in the world". Certainly, it lacks the elegance and social life which you would expect from many of Europe's great capitals. Norway is full of contrasts. It is highly civilised, with one of the highest standards of living in the world and well-developed social services. Although there is a housing shortage, there is a general lack of overcrowding and slums.

At the first opportunity, most town-dwellers get away to the lonely fjords and windswept mountains. There they enjoy skiing, hiking, sailing, swimming, hunting and fishing—practically every man and woman, boy and girl, is an expert in some or all of these sports. At an early age they achieve a skill that would astonish those living in other parts of the world.

A *hytta* is a roughly furnished wooden holiday home far away on an island or in a remote valley. Most Norwegian

A mountain *hytta* on the Sognefjell

families have a *hytta* where they spend as much of their free time as possible. They cook over paraffin lamps or wood-fed stoves; they wash in the nearest stream and it is here, too, that they do their washing-up after meals. After a day in the open air they gather round log fires for a long evening of song, dance and talking. The Norwegians love to sing and there are choirs in every town; their members are usually distinguished by the

17

coloured caps with tassels which they wear. It is a simple, healthy life but one which the average Norwegian would not exchange for all the riches in the world.

In spite of its breathtaking beauty and the seeming leisureliness of its people, life in Norway has always been hard and opportunities few and far between. Because of this, countries like Great Britain, France and America attract the more adventurous youngsters who dream of making their fortunes. Many become sailors; Norwegian ships and seamen are to be found in every major port in the world. Others have sought new homes abroad as emigrants, married and raised families. Today, in almost every part of the globe are found tall, well-built, fair-haired Norwegians who have left their native shores in search of new lives.

Oslo

Oslo, the capital city of Norway, lies at the northern tip of a long fjord, with a score of islands in front and craggy, tree-covered slopes dotted with bright little wooden houses and farmsteads behind.

The Oslo fjord is one of the busiest in Scandinavia, and a great deal of shipping travels to and from the capital. There

A view of Oslo from Oslo fjord—note the shipping in the harbour

are car ferries to Denmark and Germany, timber barges, modern ocean-going liners and large oil tankers. During the fine summer days every little creek and inlet is packed with small craft: sailing- and rowing-boats, canoes and motor-boats. The less adventurous may go by leisurely steamer or hydrofoil to the open-air restaurants, safe bathing beaches and small villages along the shores of the fjord.

On the three sides of Oslo there are stretches of rolling woodland dotted here and there with lakes. This area of forest and open moorland is known as the *Oslomarka*, or "Oslo field". On the east it is called the *Østmarka*, on the north the *Nordmarka*, and on the west the *Vestmarka*. Because of the Norwegians' passionate love of the open air every encourage-ment is given by the authorities to the preservation of large areas round the capital for recreation and relaxation. No new building is allowed in Oslo *Nordmarka*.

The summer in Norway is short so that people make the most of the bright sunshine. The winter is long and dismal. November is dark and wet; but then comes the frost and snow and the entire land is transformed from Nordic gloom to brilliant white under a cloudless blue sky. From the middle of December the snow is deep and crisp enough for skiing. Every weekend scores of happy Norwegians, dressed in gaily-coloured sweaters and anoraks, make for the skiing grounds a short distance from the city centre. The climax of the winter season is Holmenkollen Day held in February. This is the only day in the year when the largest ski-jump in the world at

Holmenkollen, just outside Oslo, is used. Before over 100,000 spectators, skiers from all over the world compete in the various trials of skill and daring.

Spring comes late in Norway: in May in the south, in June in the north. When winter ends, the dismal landscape suddenly comes to life and takes on new colour. From May onwards there is no night in Oslo—only a few hours of gentle twilight. Almost before the snows have begun to melt flowers are springing up. After the bleakness of winter people want to get out into the sun once again; so almost every other day in May is a public holiday. During the winter the *Oslomarka* is a favourite skiing ground; for the rest of the year it is a popular place for rambling and picnics.

The actual city of Oslo is not very large although the *Oslo-marka* makes it one of the largest cities in the world with regards to actual area. Although the woodlands and fjord are so close together, the middle of Oslo is as busy as any other capital. Oslo's main street, Karl Johans Gate (*Gate*, pronounced like the English *garter*, means street) contains many of the city's most important buildings and stretches nearly a mile (1·5 kilometres). At one end there is the *Slott* or Royal Palace, a square white building. Children may be seen skiing and tobogganing in the park. In spring the palace park is a mass of lilac blossom and its heady scent floats over the city. At the other end of the street is the East Railway Station. Between these two landmarks are the Parliament building where Norway's National Assembly meets, and, almost facing

The National Theatre, Oslo

each other across Karl Johan, the University and the National
Theatre. In the theatre, as well as modern plays, there are
regular performances of plays by Norway's best-known
dramatists: Henrik Ibsen (1828–1906) and Bjørnstjerne
Bjørnson (1832–1910). One of the most striking features of
Oslo is that everything is so close together. Everything—

trade, shipping, government, industry, and entertainment—
goes on side by side.

The buildings in Oslo present a strange mixture in age,
style and architecture. There are late nineteenth-century
houses in stone as well as up-to-date concrete and glass office
blocks. In the suburbs there are modern seven- or eight-storey
blocks of flats and brightly painted little wooden houses. Many
of the streets are very narrow and winding. The blue-and-
white trams go clattering round the sharp corners of these
thoroughfares.

The Cathedral is on *Stortorvet*, a market square with a fruit
and flower market. The present church was completed in 1699
but has been restored several times since then; the present
interior dates from 1849–50. Inside it is light and airy, with
fine stained-glass windows, a pulpit dating from 1699 and
brilliant ceiling paintings, illustrating Biblical stories. There is
a private box for the Royal Family. The Vår Frelsers Church
(Church of Our Saviour) became Oslo's Cathedral in 1950.
The state religion of Norway is Lutheran (Protestant) to
which about ninety-six per cent of the population belong.

Oslo was founded in the year 1050 by the Viking King Harold
Hardrada (the Hard-Ruler). Sixteen years later he was
defeated and killed by King Harold of England at the battle
of Stamford Bridge. Before 1050 there was a trading settlement
at the foot of the Ekeberg hill on the eastern side of the fjord.
Then, in about the year 1300, King Håkon V had a fortress

Oslo's City Hall

built on a rocky point of land jutting into the inner port; it was used as a royal residence until 1380. At this time, Oslo replaced the town of Trondheim as the capital of Norway, and King Håkon took up residence in his new fortress, Akershus Castle. This is the most impressive of Norway's medieval fortresses. Several of the halls—they are still used for state banquets and balls—are hung with ancient tapestries which have been woven from *spelsau* wool, which comes from crossbred Norwegian and Icelandic sheep.

A short distance from Akershus Castle and close to where the shrimp boats tie up at the quayside, there is a huge, twin-towered building of red brick. This is Oslo's fine City Hall, opened officially in 1950—the 900th anniversary of the city's foundation.

Frogner Park in Oslo is one of the show-places of the capital. It has a heated open-air swimming-pool and a magnificent rose garden. The main attraction, however, is an area which contains 150 statues in stone, iron and bronze, the work of the Norwegian sculptor Gustav Vigeland (1869-1943). They represent the story of man from birth to death and took the sculptor thirty years' work to complete. But even so it is hard to imagine how he could have done so much in the time.

The work of Gustav Vigeland which attracts many visitors to the Frogner Park in Oslo

A quarter of an hour by bus or boat from the City Hall quay is Bygdøy. This is a delightful peninsula with fields and country lanes studded with wild flowers during the summer months. Here is Oslo's open-air Folk Museum. This consists of groups of old farms, a church and over one hundred houses collected from different parts of the country. These are arranged in wooded clearings, and each house is furnished according to the period in which it was built. The collection includes a twelfth-century stave church and a small eighteenth-century Norwegian town as well as a reconstruction of Henrik Ibsen's study.

Stave churches are extremely old. They are built of wood and got their name from the pillars or staves which form the main supports of the building. Christianity established itself in Norway about A.D. 1030, and during the next three hundred years over one thousand stave churches were built. Today, only about twenty-five remain: the rest have been destroyed by fire or decay.

A short distance from the Folk Museum is a special building to house Norway's greatest treasures—the Viking ships. These funeral-ships, which once contained the bodies of Viking chieftains, were excavated from burial mounds on the shores of the Oslo fjord. They date from about the ninth century. A barrel of apples found in one of the boats contained several apples in good condition—after one thousand years!

The burial chamber of the Gokstad ship is believed to have contained the bones of a chief, Oseberg, and the Viking Queen

A stave church—one of the few which still remain in the Norwegian countryside

Åsa. With their dead, the Vikings buried jewellery, ornaments and utensils which they believed would be useful in the after-life. The Gokstad and Oseberg ships contained a rich collection of such articles. These are typical of the Viking ships, with beautiful slender lines, built for speed yet tough enough to withstand violent storms or lengthy sea voyages.

On the point of Bygdøy peninsula which juts out into the fjord, there are three more buildings comprising the Norwegian Maritime Museum. There is a fine collection of old boats

A Viking ship in the museum at Bygdøy

and Lapp canoes. The Kon-Tiki Museum houses the original balsa-wood raft on which, in 1947, the scientists Thor Heyerdahl and five companions drifted with the currents over five thousand miles (eight thousand kilometres) across the Pacific Ocean from Peru to Polynesia. In 1969, Heyerdahl set out again, this time in a boat made from papyrus, to test the theory that the ancient Egyptians could have reached America. The boat had to be abandoned, but not before Heyerdahl had proved the theory possible.

The third building contains the *Fram*, the ship used by the Norwegian scientist and explorer Fridtjof Nansen in his attempt to reach the North Pole (1893–1896). In 1910, the *Fram* was used again, this time by another Norwegian explorer, Roald Amundsen. On December 14th, 1911, Amundsen was the first man to reach the South Pole.

The Mountains

Over three-quarters of the total land area of Norway is covered by towering mountain ranges. Wherever you go the mountains are always visible; there is always a peak or a ridge on the horizon, mist-shroulded and mysterious, or sun-crowned against a startlingly blue sky.

The Norwegians have a passionate love for the mountains. When Norway was ruled by Denmark and the townspeople spoke Danish, it was the people of the mountain valleys who spoke the old Norwegian language and guarded the customs of the country.

Norwegian, like Danish and Swedish, is a branch of the Germanic language. There are three forms of the Norwegian language in the country: *Riksmål* is the literary language which is spoken in the towns by the majority of people; *Landsmål* is the dialect of the country districts. For most of this century purists have been fighting a battle for the official introduction of *Nynorsk*, based on *Landsmål*, which they claim is less subject to the influence of German and Danish than *Riksmål*. In the secondary schools, *Nynorsk* is now taught and it is also used for official documents. Most townspeople, however (apart per-

The fertile Flam Valley with snow-coverd mountains in the background

haps from those at school) still speak *Riksmål* or "ordinary" Norwegian.

During the last war, the mountains of Norway played a vital part in the guerilla warfare. Many a Norwegian saboteur owed his life and freedom to some mountain hideout where the Germans could not find or reach him.

For nearly eight months of the year the mountains are entirely snowbound. But in June the thaw comes and from then until well into September the mountains are crowded by holidaymakers.

During the winter months everything is quiet and still except for the faint rustle of shifting snow and the sudden stampede of a herd of wild reindeer in the distance. With the return of spring the harsh outlines of the rocks and the intense blue of the sky are reflected in thousands of lakes and small pools. Everywhere there is the scent of damp mosses, heather and wild mountain flowers.

According to old Norwegian legends the mountains are peopled by fierce giants and trolls. (Trolls are misshapen, stunted creatures who carry off young girls to their sinister lairs beneath the mountains.) But, say the legends, they are only dangerous after dark. It is easy to imagine sharp and cunning faces in the twisted shapes of rocks when the sun dips below the rim of the horizon.

Thousands of Norwegians all over the country spend their summer holidays, beginning in June, in long walking trips in the mountains. There are hundreds of networks of paths to guide the walkers. On most nights people stay at simple *hytte* where the cost of a bed is very cheap. However, most people carry sleeping-bags and, if the weather is fine, they spend the night in the open. But, even at midsummer, the nights become very cold.

In the mountains there is always something to see. There are many plants. The ground is covered with mosses and lichens, and the lakes are fringed with white bog-cotton grass. In places, too, there are dense tufts of low-lying plants: rose-tinted heaths, saxifrages and various species of white- and blue-blossomed Arctic plants. There are also clear mountain lakes, foaming waterfalls and fast-flowing rivers. Sometimes the route passes through dark woods; sometimes across a rocky mountain waste and over glaciers.

After a long day's walking, the red-painted mountain *hytta* with its fluttering Norwegian flag is a welcome sight indeed. Mountain food is especially delicious. Appetites are enormous after a long day in the open air. There may be hot broth or *fruktsuppe* (a cold soup made from a mixture of different fruits) followed by brown river trout, or roast reindeer steaks with cranberry sauce. For dessert there is *multekrem*, golden yellow cloudberries with thick whipped cream. In the lower valleys, where there are dairy cattle, the country dish of *rømmekolle* is frequently served. This is curds (the thick part of milk which separates from the watery part) mixed with a little cream. During the day many people carry with them *smørbrød* of *geitost*, a sweet cheese made from goats' milk.

In the evenings, people make their own entertainment at the mountain *hytta*. There may be community singing, or folk dancing. Norway has a very rich tradition of folk music, from the oldest surviving type of *kjempeviser*, the words of one of the old epic-lyrical poems sung by a leader, with everyone joining in the chorus, to the old religious songs and the many dances and bridal marches. There are several native instruments, including the *lur*, the *selje* (flute) and the *bukke* (horn)—all wind instruments—and the zither-like *langeleik*. But the most famous of the Norwegian instruments is the *Hardingfele*, or

Hardanger violin. It is a violin with two sets of strings, one mounted above the other, the lower set vibrating when the upper strings are played. It became known in Western Norway in the seventeenth century. A farmer, worried for some time by what he thought was magic music coming from the mountainside, eventually plucked up courage to investigate and found a local farmhand playing this weird instrument, which sounds similar to the Scottish bagpipes. The folk music played on the Hardanger violin is not written down but handed down from one fiddler (or *spelemann*) to the next.

A mountain *hytta* flying the Norwegian flag

The Norwegian Touring Club has built a great many *hytte* where hundreds of Norwegians and travellers from other lands may spend a cheap holiday among the sun-dappled mountains. These simple little living-huts are extremely comfortable. Good food, interesting conversation and a blazing fire eclipse whatever is happening outside. The wind might howl and the temperature fall to many degrees below zero but this is quickly forgotten in the kindly company of friends. Outside, endless snow-dunes in ever-changing forms flow away into the vast, empty stillness, under the burning sun. The wind carves weird and grotesque shapes in the packed snow.

The western fjord country is a holiday area popular both with Norwegians and with visitors from abroad. During the summer months the many hotels, camping huts and farms are filled to overflowing. There is something to suit every taste: salmon and sea-trout fishing, walks in superb mountain scenery, bathing, boating, water-skiing, and exploration trips on the leisurely fjord steamers.

Eastland and Southland

Norway is divided officially into nineteen counties or *fylker*. As in Great Britain, there is a friendly rivalry between those people who live in the north and those in the south. An Eastlander is a man who lives in the south-eastern part of Norway, between the mountains and the Swedish frontier. The western valleys form the Westland; and the south coast the Southland. It is far more common in Norway to speak of a man as a Northlander or an Eastlander than as a resident of a particular *fylker*.

The Eastland, which includes Oslo, is the richest region of Norway. Here are the great valleys of Gudbrandsda (with a fine tradition of folk art), Hallingdal, Numedal and Østerdal with their towering tree-covered flanks and gentle fields. (Østerdal runs almost parallel with the Swedish frontier. The River Glomma, longest and one of the most important rivers in Norway, flows through it.)

In this region there are a great number of small farms devoted mainly to raising cows, sheep, goats and horses. Each farm has a large, two-storey wooden barn; the upper part is used for storing hay and fodder, the lower part for the housing of animals in winter. In Norway, farming is a difficult job. For six months of the year the farmer can do little because his fields are buried deep in drifts of snow. All he can do is sit and wait patiently for the thaw to come.

When spring and summer arrive, the days are long and the crops grow at tremendous speed in the warm moist ground. The land must be ploughed and the crops sown and harvested. All this must take place in a much shorter time than in Western Europe where the seasons are much longer.

In the valleys the grass is rich but there is not much of it. In early June the farmer or his sons take the sheep, cows and goats to the upland pastures of the temporary farm high on the plateau. They return to the main farm in September after the hay has been cut and hung between poles to dry in the sun. Nowadays, the farmers are experimenting with other types of cattle food so that it is no longer a necessity to keep a *seter*, or small farm, up on the plateau. Many of the *seters* have become holiday homes.

Few farmers in Norway are rich; the work is too hard and uncertain for that. But they are generous and hospitable people who find pleasure in entertaining complete strangers in their homes. These might be newly-built, gleaming with fresh paint and varnish, or they might be several hundred years old, built of logs placed one on top of another with a thick turf roof, with mosses and wild flowers growing on top.

Norwegians are great home-lovers and they spend much thought and imagination on the decoration and furnishing of their homes. Inside most farmhouses is a wealth of strong tables and chairs, chests and cupboards, clocks and lamps. The

37

A typically blond
Norwegian girl
wearing a colourful
local costume

heating is provided by large iron stoves; and the walls are
frequently hung with attractive woollen mats. The general
effect is one of warmth and comfort.

In spite of the scarcity of good grass, Norway produces more
milk than she needs. Much of the surplus is exported in the
form of cheese, mainly to Great Britain and Far Eastern
countries such as Japan.

During the long winter months the Norwegian farmers
spend their time in decorating their homes and making
wooden ornaments. Like their German cousins they are skilled
woodcarvers and painters. Their wives make their traditional
local costumes—long dresses, tight bodices and embroidered

aprons. One of the most attractive is the costume of the Hardanger area, with its red bonnet and bodice, embroidered blouse, and white apron over a long black skirt. The men wear knee-breeches and short waistcoats. Each district has its own distinctive style and colouring. Such costumes are compulsory wear for special occasions.

One of the most colourful of these celebrations is a country wedding. The young bride, in an elaborate head-dress of silver and seed pearls, the bridegroom, families, relatives and friends, all in national costume, ride to the church. The village *spelemann* scratches out a lively country dance and a wooden beer-bowl is handed round. The wedding service is conducted by a Lutheran minister in a long black gown and white bands. In the church the women sit on one side, the men on the other. Afterwards there is feasting, drinking, dancing and singing. The festivities continue well into the evening when the lamps are lit in the cottage windows. On such occasions the feasting has been known to last for three whole days!

The plain of Hedmark, lies by Norway's largest lake, Mjøsa, where the Gudbrandsdal and Østerdal meet. The fields slope steeply down to the water's edge. The hundred-year-old paddle-steamer, *Skibladner*, plies back and forth between the industrial town of Hamar and the village of Lillehammer.

Lillehammer, one of the best-known holiday centres in Norway, is surrounded by beautiful pine and spruce forests. It lies at the point where lake, valley and mountain join. On one

Norwegian dancers in local traditional costume entertaining on board ship at Bergen

side are fertile fields and farms; on the other is a ski-lift leading up to a world of rock and snow. The wooden houses and carefully tended gardens seem to cling to the hillsides. Half the streets in the village are so steep that they seem almost vertical. If you climb high enough you will arive at *Maihaugen*, the most impressive museum in Norway. The museum comprises a private collection of old buildings from the Gudbrandsdal, founded in 1887 by Dr. Anders Sandvig. They are arranged as a complete village and show the development of the Norwegian farm from its earliest days down to the present.

Gudbrandsdal and Hallingdal are farming valleys. Østerdal, the longest and easternmost valley, is largely forested. Here the lumberjacks work in extreme cold and loneliness. Timber is cut during the winter, and the lumberjacks spend long months deep in the forests, living in primitive huts and putting up with conditions that seem almost unbearable. The logs are trimmed and dragged down to the river to wait for the spring thaw, which will carry them down to the timber mills of Sarpsborg and Moss by the sea.

Trondheim is not part of the Eastland, but the two have been closely linked by a railway running over the Dovre Mountains. Today there are two railways between Oslo and Trondheim; one goes up Gudbrandsdal, over the ridges of

A winter street scene in Lillehammer on Lake Mjosa

Dovre, the other follows Østerdal, passing the little town of Røros, with its turf-thatched houses and worked-out copper mines. Two or three times a day trains wheeze along each route, stopping for ten minutes or so at every town and village so that the engine can gather enough steam for the next long haul.

Another railway leads from Oslo to the Southland, passing through the farming valleys and timber rivers of Telemark to Kristiansand and Stavanger. Some of the coaches have observation platforms, with iron gates, where you can stand in the open air and watch the lakes and trees go rattling by.

Because of the nature of the land it costs a great deal of money to build railways in Norway; fjords and gorges must be spanned by bridges, and the walls of mountains blasted out to make tunnels. As there is a shortage of coal but plenty of electricity, the lines are electrified wherever possible. The year 1954 was the hundredth anniversary of the opening of Norway's first railway line. The line was built from the capital northwards to the village of Eidsvoll, and was constructed so that timber for export could be brought cheaply from the country districts to the port of Oslo. At the centenary celebrations, an old train was brought out of retirement from the Railway Museum at Hamar and driven to Oslo and Bergen. The *Caroline* was made in Great Britain in the Newcastle factory started by George Stephenson. His son Robert also became a famous engineer and, in 1851, under his leadership, a firm of British contractors started to lay the Oslo to Eidsvoll line. Most of Norway's railways are in the southeast; in fact, well over three-quarters of the total railway network is south of Trondheim.

The main Southland railway hardly touches the coast at all, and it is much more fun to travel by branchline down to Arendal or Grimstad. This particular journey is usually by a single autocar, with the driver sitting next to the passengers and chatting with them. The driver will stop anywhere you ask him, possibly at a country path or a garden gate.

Grimstad (home of the great dramatist Henrik Ibsen), Kragero (a seaside town popular with artists), Tvedestrand and Risør are the loveliest towns found in the Southland. The white-painted, red-roofed houses, each surrounded by flowers, perch on rocky slopes rising steeply from the sea. Each house faces in a different direction and the streets and alleyways are crooked and narrow.

Unlike the people in other parts of Norway every Southlander has the advantage of unlimited opportunity to enjoy the sun and the sea, which are as warm in the summer as in the Mediterranean. This is a popular tourist area and the local people make their living catering for the thousands of holidaymakers who flock to the area every year. There are *hytte* on every island and promontory.

The southern part of Norway is one of the most important areas for the growing of vegetables: carrots and, under glass, tomatoes and cucumbers. These are especially welcomed by the people living in the snow-bound north. Stavanger, the capital of Rogaland and Norway's fourth largest town, lies close to this vegetable-producing area. The Norwegian novelist and playwright, Alexander Kjelland (1849–1906) was an inhabitant of Stavanger.

This is a wonderful part of Norway where nobody bothers to hurry and the buses and paddle-steamers are nearly always late, because half the passengers would miss them if they were on time.

Holiday-time makes this region one of the most outstanding in Europe. A fishing trip on the mirror-like sea; as few clothes as possible; sunbathing all day and a swim at evening; a roaring bonfire on the rocks at midnight, a sing-song while the steaks and sausages spit on the glowing charcoal—this is the life of the Southland, for a few short summer months, before the fog and cold of winter begin.

Old wooden buildings in Stavanger

Trondheim and the North

Norway's third largest city is Trondheim. It is older than either Oslo or Bergen (the two largest cities) and was originally the capital, then called Nidaros. Built on a triangle of land it is almost surrounded by the River Nid. Trondheim is the centre of the encircling farm lands. It belongs to neither the Westland, the Eastland nor the North.

This ancient town was founded in A.D. 997 by the Viking King Olav Trygvason, the eleventh-century Norse adventurer, who discovered part of America when he was driven off course on his way to Greenland. He also spent some time in England, returning to Norway in the year 995, determined to convert his countrymen to Christianity. His task was finally completed by King Olav Haraldson, whose gallant efforts ended in his death in 1030 at the Battle of Stiklestad against King Canute of England. According to an old legend, a clear spring gushed from the ground where King Olav's body was laid to rest in Trondheim. Believing this to be a miracle the local inhabitants built a little chapel there which quickly became a place of pilgrimage. Olav was later canonised and became Norway's patron saint.

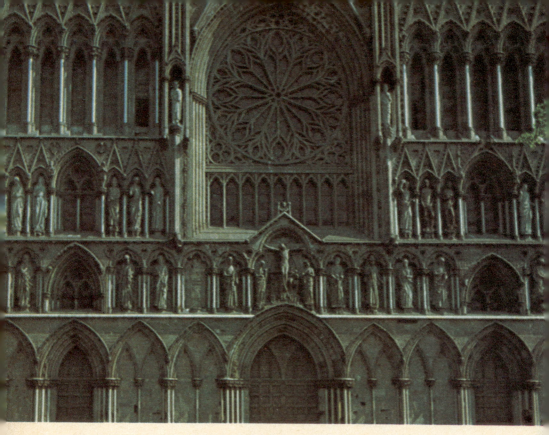

The Gothic cathedral at Trondheim

Trondheim is a clean, pleasant town with broad streets and some fine old houses. At the southern end of *Munkegaten* ("Monks' Street") is the grey-stone, half-Norman, half-Gothic Nidaros Cathedral founded in about 1150. It is the most impressive cathedral in Norway and was built to commemorate the death of St Olav. It stands on the site of the original commemorative chapel; St Olav's well can still be seen outside the cathedral. The magnificent rose window and stone fan vaulting alone make a visit worth while.

Halfway between the cathedral and the fjord is a market place with a gigantic statue of St Olav. Here, in the market place there are fruit, vegetable and fish stalls; it is an exciting bustle of activity and a babble of voices and sounds. Behind the statue lies the *Stiftsgården*. This is the present king's northern palace, built between 1660–1670; it is the largest wooden building in Norway. Along the River Nid stand old warehouses dating from 1708. These are raised on stilts and each is painted a different colour.

The city has a very fine technical university (*Norges Tekniske Høgskole*), steelworks, yards for building fishing-boats, a deep-freezing works and a brisling cannery. Brislings, small fish similar to sardines, are about six inches (fifteen centimetres) in length.

Trondheim is an important centre of communications and a port of call for the coastal express steamers. It is also a starting-point of cruises to North Cape and the Midnight Sun.

Trondheim has a long and exciting history, and was the scene of several fierce battles in the twelfth century. In the year 1564 it was occupied by the Swedes. At the Peace of Roskilde in 1658 the city and the surrounding area was given to Sweden. But it was recaptured by the Norwegian forces later that same year.

About twenty miles (thirty-two kilometres) east of Trondheim is a village with the extraordinary name of Hell. This is situated at a junction on Norway's fifth and last mainline railway. From here the line divides into two, one branch going east to Stockholm in Sweden, the other north to the Arctic Circle. Nine hours after leaving the fine city of Trondheim the train crosses the Arctic Circle. The countryside is *tundra*—a mixture of lonely moors and stone-strewn wastes. This is the "Land of the Midnight Sun".

The Nordland railway follows the fjord, then continues along a valley stretching northeastwards between two mountain ranges. Farms and wooded slopes rise on either side, until the line drops down again to the sea at Mosjøen and Mo i Rana. Mo is a modern town set in magnificent surroundings. It has one of the largest iron and steel plants in the world. From here it is easy to reach the Svartis Glacier, the second largest glacier in Norway or the fantastic Grønli Grotto, a 457-mile (735-kilometre) long cavern with an impressive underground waterfall.

The whole vast stretch of *Nord Norge* ("North Norway"), from just north of Mo i Rana, lies within the Arctic Circle, yet even here the harbours are ice-free all the year round and trees grow further north than anywhere else in the world. The surprisingly temperate climate is due to the Gulf Stream which flows along the coast. From Mo i Rana the Nordland railway connects with Bodø and Trondheim, and the highway is the main route to the far north.

Bodø is the county town of Nordland and a port. It is the first town beyond the Arctic Circle where the midnight sun is visible—from early June to early July. The town has been completely rebuilt since the last war. The modern cathedral

(1956) has an unusual sealskin-covered font, a lovely rose window representing the Northern Lights and pews made from American pine. Near Bodø is a narrow channel between the mainland and the island of Straum. Twice a day the tide is forced through this narrow strait taking with it enormous numbers of fish. This is known as the Saltstraumen Eddy.

From Bodø northwards, for a period during summer, the sun never sets, and in winter the sun never rises above the horizon. In the far north in midwinter nothing more than a faint twilight is achieved during the day but, as if in compensation, there is the brilliant Aurora Borealis, or Northern Lights in the sky—a wonderful display of bands of light produced in the upper atmosphere. The summers are glowing, with vivid colour everywhere, perhaps most of all on the high Finnmark Plateau. Up here, on this wild and lonely tundra, the rare *multer* or wild cloudberries grow in large quantities. These berries are yellowy orange in colour and have a slightly acid flavour.

North of Bodø *Road 50* is the only land route of importance. It runs the whole length of Norway from Oslo to Kirkenes, a distance of some 800 miles (1,287 kilometres) to the Russian frontier.

The two most important towns in the Nordland are Trømso and Hammerfest which both stand on islands. Trømso is called the "Capital of the North". It is an important cod-fishing port. It is also a departure-point for expeditions to Greenland and Newfoundland in quest of seals which are

Hammerfest harbour

killed for their beautiful and valuable skins. Nearly 250 miles (402 kilometres) north of the Arctic Circle, Trømso is encircled by snow-capped mountains. The ancient wooden houses, the narrow streets and the horse-drawn carts make it one of the most attractive towns in Norway. In the harbour are found ships from many nations.

Hammerfest is the most northerly town in the world. During the last war it was completely destroyed, except for a little chapel. It has now been rebuilt and has a fine fishing-port and harbour. On the far side of the harbour is the Meridian Stone, marking the first international measurement of the world's exact size (1819–52). Hammerfest stands on Kvaløy, separated by a narrow strait from the mainland. The coastal scenery is very rugged and is the home of thousands of seabirds.

Coastal steamers maintain a daily service between the towns and villages dotted along the coast from Bergen and Trondheim to Kirkeness. These steamers keep up their work throughout the year. They establish an essential link with the little communities, bringing them everything they need in exchange for the fish which goes all over the world.

The Lofoten islands are the hub of the northern fishing industry. From Bodø it is only six hours by coastal steamer to

North Cape—the most northerly point of the European coast—has spectacular sunrises and sunsets, like this one

Svolvaer, the chief fishing village of the Lofotens. From a distance, the islands look like a sheer wall of high mountains stretching for some sixty miles (ninety-six kilometres). It is here that great shoals of cod come to breed each spring and here, in every village, fishing-boats from the whole coast gather for the "harvest of the sea". The cod is exported all over the world. The fishing-grounds are so close to the coastal filleting plants that the fish is delivered, filleted and frozen, within a few hours of being caught. The traditional way the Norwegians have of drying fish is to behead, gut and wash them, and then hang them on racks for up to three months.

On some of the Lofoten islands and in several other places in the Nordland, the collecting of down from the eider duck provides additional work for the fishermen and their families. The down is sent by fjord steamer to Bodø, Trondheim and Tromso where it is prepared for pillows and eiderdown quilts.

Northwards lies the modern iron-ore port of Narvik. The port is always busy handling the shipment of ore from the Swedish mines just beyond the frontier. Narvik was the scene of a famous battle during the last war, and the iron ore quay and installations were blown up by the Germans. The Lofoten Railway, the most northerly electrified line in the world, is used chiefly to bring the iron ore from the Swedish mines to the port at Narvik.

The coast of Europe reaches its northernmost point in the majestic cliffs of the North Cape. Round the coast from the North Cape to the Russian border there are fishing villages and towns as well as Vardø, the county town of the desolate Finnmark, and Kirkenes with its iron-ore mines. In some parts a snowmobile service delivers mail and essential supplies when the weather makes more normal deliveries impossible.

The Northlanders are quiet and reserved. Their lives are closely regulated by the periods of light and darkness. In February when the sun first rises above the horizon everyone celebrates joyfully while during the summer the Midnight Sun bathes the sea and land with golden light.

Because of the harshness and uncertainty of the climate the people rely very much on the help and companionship of friends and neighbours. For example, working conditions in a factory may be organised by the workers themselves who each buy shares in the factory out of their pay. This idea is now being adopted in other parts of the country. Gradually the Nordland is being developed with the help of money paid in taxes by the more affluent regions. No longer is it the most neglected part of Norway.

The Lapps

The rapid technical development and progress found in the Nordland contrasts with the life of the nomadic Lapp. There are some 20,000 Lapps in Norway, many of whom live on the desolate and treeless wastes of Finnmark. Their beginnings are not known but it is believed that they originated from the north-western part of Russia and from the middle basin of the River Volga. They belong to the Mongol race. They are short and thick-set, with high cheekbones, dark hair and olive skins unlike their tall, blue-eyed, fair-haired Norwegian countrymen.

They have not changed their way of life since they first began taming huge herds of wild reindeer and following them on their annual migrations to the coastlands in summer and back to the mountain plateaus of Finnmark in winter, nearly seven hundred years ago.

Their living conditions are simple and uncomfortable. They live in rough tents rather like Indian wigwams with a hole in the top to let out the smoke from the fire, which not only

Two Lapps wearing their traditional warm and colourful clothes, including the unusual four-pointed cap stuffed with eiderdown

supplies warmth for the family but also serves as a means of cooking. Like the Eskimoes, their needs are few and undemanding; they eat reindeer-meat—a vast quantity at each meal—and wild berries which they gather from the stunted bushes of the uninhabited wastes of the *vidder*.

Men, women and children all wear similar clothes: reindeer-skin boots and leggings, a thick fur coat in winter and a *kofte* or blue woollen tunic in summer, and an unusual four-pointed cap stuffed with eiderdown to make the points stick out. The caps and tunics are brightly decorated with coloured ribbons and rosettes; for special occasions a silk scarf is added to the outfit. The Lapps never take their clothes off in winter; to do so would mean freezing to death in the bitter Finnmark climate. During the biting months of winter they sleep huddled together for warmth on the tent floor round the piled fire.

The reindeer are half-tame, half-wild creatures. They live together in herds often numbering many hundreds. During the summer months they live on grass. In winter they feed on the pale green moss found growing on the rocks and under bushes. They use their long antlers to dig away the deep snow in search of food. Each Lapp owns anything from a few hundred to several thousand reindeer, from which much of their income derives. Most Lapps dislike and distrust money besides the fact that they have little need for it. What they earn by selling reindeer meat and skins they usually spend on coffee, sugar, tobacco and cloth. They take an almost fierce pride in being entirely independent of western civilization although they will occasionally make use of it. Kautokeino is a Lapp village on the mountain plateau. The work of Kautokeino's Lapp silversmiths finds its way all over the world.

In theory, the Lapps are citizens of Norway, Sweden and Finland. But in practice they are very much their own masters and follow their heads in everything. Each family has the hereditary right to graze their herds of reindeer on a certain part of the wild *vidder*. Because of their utter contentment with

These Lapp schoolboys at Kautokeino in Finnmark are as interested as boys the world over in cars and motorcycles. In spite of their traditional dress they are very up-to-date

life they quarrel rarely either between themselves or with the Norwegians. Keeping very much to themselves they cause little or no embarrassment to the Norwegian Government who are more than content to let the Lapps live in their time-honoured fashion.

For eighteen weeks of the year the Lapp children go to school in Kautokeino. These are boarding-schools. The dis-

57

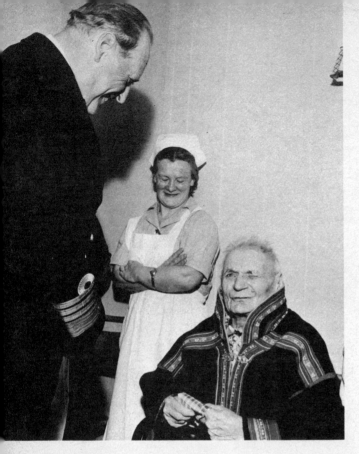

The King of
Norway, well-
known for his
friendliness and
informality,
chatting with an
old Lapp

tances are much too great to permit easy travelling to and
from school each day. But the young Lapps' real schooling—
the basic skills necessary for survival—takes place on the
sweeping *vidder*, where they quickly learn how to lasso a
reindeer, harness it to a snow sledge, or kill and cut it up into
steaks. It is a tough upbringing with none of the comforts and
amusements youngsters expect in other parts of the world but
the young Lapps seem healthy and contented enough. With
their families the children speak Lappish (a language very

similar to Finnish), but at boarding-school they learn to read and speak Norwegian fluently like any other child in Norway.

In spite of their determination to resist it, civilization is slowly changing the lives of many Lapps. Hundreds of Lapps have given up their nomadic life for a more settled routine as farmers, labourers and shop assistants. On the Finnmark Plateau, near the Finnish frontier, is the town of Karasjok, with a population of under a thousand. Some of the Karasjok Lapps are still nomadic, owning herds of reindeer; others live in Norwegian-type houses. The majority of the houses in Karasjok are new because there was little left of historic interest in Finnmark after the last war.

But there are still thousands of Lapps who prefer the hardships of the *vidder*; they are proud of their freedom and independence, and have little respect for those who have forsaken the ancient ways of their ancestors for the comforts of town life. They can see no reason to change their way of life, and nor can the Norwegian Government. The Lapps have one great advantage over other minority groups: they live in a land which no one else wants.

Bergen and the Western Fjords

Bergen, on the south-west coast, is the second largest city of Norway. It is one of the main arrival ports for passengers by sea from Great Britain, the Continent of Europe and America. The city was founded in 1070 by King Olav Kyrre and all the early kings were crowned there. Bergen's prosperity has developed so much that it has become the biggest seafaring and trading area in the country. It is the chief port of Norway.

Literally, the name Bergen or Bjørgvin means "the meadow by the mountain". This is a very apt description. As the train from Oslo approaches Bergen, the track drops steeply from the mountain plateau of the Hardangervidder—covered with cranberry and bilberry bushes—into a narrow valley full of lush growth. Trees, flowers and grasses make a pleasing contrast to the orderly fir-trees and rugged countryside of Oslo Nordmarka.

Bergen, with a population of some 120,000, is a particularly beautiful city. Its bright little wooden houses painted yellow, green and brown are surrounded by flower-filled gardens.

A view of Bergen

Down by the Hansa quay, high gabled buildings lean towards each other across the streets like those in medieval pictures. Lamps are often seen burning in the lower windows of these houses all day long because they are too close together to catch the daylight. Many of the houses date from 1916 when they were rebuilt after fire gutted most of the old city. The last war also had its effect on the city, especially in 1944 when an ammunition ship was blown up in the harbour.

Bergen, seen from Mount Fløyen

In spite of its old-world appearance, Bergen is very much a modern industrial city. The university city of Bergen is built on the slopes of seven mountains which enclose it on the north, east and south; to the west there lies a necklace of islands. The encircling mountains on three sides make Bergen one of the finest natural harbours in the world. But the mountains trap the clouds driving from the west. This makes Bergen one of the wettest places in Norway; there are only about two weeks in the year when there is no rain.

There is a cable car service from Bergen to Mount Ulriken. And, from close by the fish market, a cable railway (*Fløybanen*) runs up the steep, birch-clad flanks of Fløyen. Far below, the city lies spread, looking very beautiful from such a height.

Fishermen from the western and northern coast right up to Finnmark make the long journey to Bergen to sell their dried cod (*klippfisk*) and to buy supplies and equipment. The fish market is a fascinating place. Besides cod, halibut, plaice, turbot, pink shrimps, haddock, hake, whiting and ling are sold to the housewives who throng the stalls. The fish are kept alive in tanks of sea-water until bought. During spring and summer, housewives also buy tuna fish steaks, and salmon, smoked or fresh. But cod still remains the most popular fish with most Norwegians. It is served in the homes of Bergen with melted butter and new potatoes—and a delicious meal it is too.

Many other west coast towns share in the important fishing trade. Kristiansund, right on the coast and built on three islands linked by bridges, Ålesund, Norway's busiest fishing port and centre of the herring fisheries, Måløy, Florø, Haugesund, Stavanger—these are the cod and herring ports. They are all little towns lost among the wild beauty of granite cliffs and barren, bird-haunted islands.

Nearly every fishing-boat in Norway is small, with a crew of between six to eight men. The season is short so full-time fishermen are rare in Norway. February and March are the busiest months. Boats from far and wide bring their catches to

Part of Bergen's busy fish market

the ports, to be dried, tinned or processed and ground into fertilizer. Profits from the sale of the fish are divided among the boat-owners and the crews. When not at sea, the fishermen cultivate strips of land along the coast or carve wooden figures of trolls and witches, which are sold in shops throughout the world.

At the end of May each year an International Festival of Music, Drama and Folklore is held at Bergen. Famous singers, musicians and conductors from all over the world come to the city. Plays by Henrik Ibsen and other Norwegian dramatists are performed at Norway's oldest theatre, Den Nationale Scene, which was founded in 1850 by the distinguished violinist Ole Bull (1810–1880) who was born in the city. There are also folk dancing displays, with the performers dressed in national costume.

Principally, the Festival is held in memory of Edvard Grieg (1843–1907), Norway's greatest composer. His music is loved and played all over the world. During his lifetime Grieg spent his winters journeying throughout Europe giving concerts of his music; in the summer, he and his wife Nina lived at Hop, just south of Bergen, in a house overlooking the superb Lake Nordås. Grieg loved his home which he called *Troldhaugen* ("Hill of Trolls"). Today, the house is a museum, furnished exactly as it was during the great composer's lifetime. Piano

The west-coast town of Alesund, Norway's busiest fishing port

A public statue
commemorating
Ole Bull, the
Norwegian
nineteenth-
century violinist

recitals are given each year on Grieg's own instrument. In the wooded garden there are two paths which slope down to the shores of Nordås. One path leads to a little red-painted summer house; it was here that Grieg did much of his composing, including orchestral music for Ibsen's poetic drama *Peer Gynt*. In the music you can hear the blizzards of winter, the violent rhythm of the waves pounding against the rocks, the sound of a clear mountain stream leaping over pebbles; it paints a wonderful picture of Norway's mountains and fjords.

The second path leads down to a narrow strip of shingle, where Grieg used to push his boat out to fish in the lake. The face of the cliff rises from the water. High up, a piece of the rock had been cut out leaving a small cavity behind. The stone slab has been replaced. It hides the ashes of those two, whose names are roughly cut on the rock: *Edvard* and *Nina*.

The fjords of western Norway are famous throughout the world. There is nothing else quite like them: gentle valleys and

The home of Edvard Grieg, near Bergen, now a museum

A view of the Sognefjord

towering rock-faces, sun-kissed waters and savage mountain blizzards. Two of the finest fjords in Norway are Sognfjord and Hardanger. Sognfjord is best approached by steamer. Gazing up at the rugged precipices the visitor is very conscious of his own insignificance. Everywhere the black rockface presses in on all sides; streams trace their courses from above, often falling from enormous heights into the water below. Tiny villages, bright with flowers, cling to the steep flanks of the fjord; there are little ledges and crevices of grass and plough-land from which the farmers manage to make a living. Life in these parts is indeed isolated and lonely.

In the fjords the traditional means of travelling is by sea. Until quite recently the only land routes were the narrow paths leading up to the *seters*, so steep that only herds of cattle could climb them with any degree of safety. But today every village has its own road which curves through the mountains from the valley floor to the plateau.

One of the valleys, Flåm, is the terminus of a little railway, the Flamsbanen, which climbs nearly 3,000 feet (912 metres) in fifty-three minutes to Myrdalon on the Oslo-Bergen rail-way. Rather than take the track on a zig-zag course over the mountain peaks, the engineers built it inside a tunnel through the mountain. The train emerges out of the mountainside beneath a gigantic waterfall, so near, indeed, that the spray spangles the carriage windows. In an hour, this unusual rail-way carries passengers, not only from valley to mountain, but from one season to another. Here is yet another example of the astonishing contrasts found in the fjords. Warm sunshine and bright flowers down by the fjord give way to deep snow and biting winds up at Myrdalon. At Finse and Mjølfjell, near by, winter sports are still in progress in June.

South of the high mountains lies Hardanger. Here the scenery, while still wild, is less awe-inspiring. It is a gentler and more welcoming country altogether; the mountains are lower, seeming to protect the farms with their comforting bulk. Steamers sail placidly across the vast sheet of calm water.

The southern arm of Hardanger is one of the most beautiful sights in Norway. The mountain slops fall one behind the other into the water, remote and peaceful. Thousands of apple trees grow along the shoreline; during May, the white

A fine view of the Flam Valley, seen from the railway

A cascading waterfall near the Hardanger Fjord

blossoms set against the deep blue of the water have a magical beauty.

There are other gentler fjords south of Hardanger, and wild ones north of Sogn. Nordfjord, Sunnfjord and Romsdalsfjord are all well worth a visit. But Hardanger, for sheer beauty and peace, is in a class of its own.

Growing Up In Norway

Beginning at a very early age Norwegian boys and girls are brought up to be hard-working, physically fit and self-reliant. Such an upbringing is necessary because life in Norway is often harsh and demanding. This attitude is best seen in the children's approach to their parents and other adults. In the Norwegian language there is no word for "sir". To say "sir" to any man is to imply that he is, in some sense, superior to the person speaking. Every Norwegian—dustman and company director, employer and employee, teacher and pupil, child and parent—treats everyone else as an equal and addresses them by surname or Christian name only. This in no way shows a lack of respect or good manners but serves to illustrate the friendliness and good nature of Norway's people. What the average Norwegian might call good manners are far more casual and relaxed than those expected in England for example. Because men and women are on an equal footing, with the same pay and job opportunities the old habits have long disappeared. It is rare in Norway to see a man give up his seat to a woman on a bus; she would not expect him to either. On the other hand, the Norwegians have several charming customs which are always observed; to forget them would be a very bad breach of basic good manners.

Off to school on a winter's day—many Norwegian children walk to school in conditions like this

During a meal whoever is serving the food and drink says to each person in turn, "*Vaersågod*"—"be so good (as to take this)." At the end of the meal, everyone stands and says to the hostess, "*Takk for maten*"—"Thank you for the food". And she replies, "*Velbekomme*"—"Hope it does you good". If you have been invited out, and happen to meet your host or hostess again during the next few days or so, you must say, "*Takk for sist*"—"Thank you for last time"; and they reply, "*I like måte*"—"The same to you".

Norwegian children learn from an early age to live in a community, for in all towns there are day nurseries, run by the municipality. These are in the open air both summer and

73

winter, as long as the weather permits, and are usually based in a public park. Going to and from the nursery the youngsters walk in single file, holding onto a rope guided by the experienced and capable *Parktante* ("park aunt").

Compulsory education starts at the age of seven and ends at the age of fifteen. The sons and daughters of rich and poor, King and commoner, all go to the same schools. These are nearly all co-educational and run by the State. There is much greater freedom between the younger generation than there used to be. School starts at 9 a.m. and finishes shortly after 2 p.m. six days a week, including Saturday. Like many of the houses in Norway, the school buildings are wooden and are painted in bright colours. Double windows help to keep out the cold and in many of the classrooms there are old-fashioned wood-burning stoves. During the winter months the children arrive on skis, with their lunch boxes strapped to their backs. In Norway there is no compulsory school uniform.

From the age of seven to thirteen years a boy or girl goes to a Junior School. From there until the age of fifteen they go to a Youth School. For those who wish to continue their education after the age of fifteen, there are two kinds of secondary schools—the *Realskole*, which gives a general three-to-four-year course to serve as a basis for specialised technical training; and the *Gymnasium* (Grammar School) for a further three years and then on to a university. To get into a *Gymnasium* boys and girls must pass examinations in four subjects: Norwegian, English, German and Mathematics.

Not surprisingly, fish in all its forms is a very popular food in Norway. This fish market has a wide variety on sale

The history, culture and institutions of Norway and the other Scandinavian countries play an important part in Norwegian education. But all schools take a lively and informed interest in foreign affairs. English is the main foreign language taught, and is compulsory in all the secondary schools.

During the winter months in particular Norwegians make the most of the short hours of light. Offices begin work at about eight-thirty in the morning and finish at four o'clock in the afternoon.

Breakfast consists of eggs, bread, several kinds of cheese, milk, fruit and cold meat or fish. The lunch break is very short—barely half an hour. Most Norwegians eat a snack which they bring with them. This is *smørbrød*, a delicious open sandwich topped by a variety of cold meats and cheeses. Dinner, or *middag*, comes soon after four o'clock and consists of vast dishes of meat or fish, potatoes and vegetables. After such a large meal the whole family take what is called "the after-dinner rest". This lasts from about five o'clock to six-thirty. During this time it is considered discourteous to visit or telephone anyone.

Norwegians are great readers, thinkers and talkers; and they love their homes intensely. They would much rather sit at home with a few close friends with a bottle of whisky or *aquavit* (potato brandy) than seek their entertainment in the towns. The family unit is of tremendous importance in Norway and children form a vital and lively part.

School starts soon after half-past eight. There are no cooked lunches in Norwegian schools but towards the middle of the morning the pupils eat their *smørbrød* which they have brought from home. In Oslo they are all given free milk and fresh fruit. Due to this policy of free milk, health among school children has been consistently high.

In Norwegian schools each class (grade) has a school day of a different length. Most nights of the week are taken up with an hour's homework, or more as pupils grow older. The school summer holiday begins in the middle of June. Norwegians take their holidays seriously; Norway was the first country in the world to establish a legal minimum of three weeks' paid holiday a year for every worker.

A classroom in one of Norway's many modern school buildings

In June, many families shut up their homes in Oslo and go to their simple country homes. These might be tucked away in some valley or perched dizzily on the shoulder of a fjord. For nearly two months this *hytta* life consists of boating, swimming and mountaineering in the bright sunshine until the beginning of autumn which comes in about the middle of August.

Norway has every reason to feel justly proud of her universities and places of higher education. Less than 200 years ago no universities existed. Today universities and colleges have been built all over the country. Oslo University, founded in 1815, has faculties of theology, history and philosophy, medicine, law, mathematics and natural science. Bergen has faculties of theology, medicine, law, natural science and the humanities. Norway's Technical High School is at Trondheim. There is a college of business administration at Bergen and state colleges of dentistry, agriculture and veterinary science at Oslo. Every boy and girl willing and able to follow a university course may do so, depending on his or her success at school examinations.

In general, university students have very little money and lead a simple life. There are few families who can afford to pay an adequate allowance so the students must borrow from the State and take holiday jobs as guides or bus drivers to earn money. "Working one's way through college" is quite as common in Norway as it is in America. State grants must be repaid by the student, often at the rate of a few kroners a month. (Norway uses the metric system for its weights, measures and coins. Prices are reckoned in krone and øre. One krone equals one hundred øre.)

Norway's university students are among some of the most hard-working in the world. They must be because competition to get into the universities is fierce. At examination time they work fantastically long hours without a break. Instead of three hours for each examination paper, as in Great Britain, they work twelve hours—from nine o'clock in the morning to nine o'clock at night. But, in spite of hard work, they still have time for relaxation and exercise in a bracing climate. The *Studenterhytta* in Nordmarka, one of the largest and best equipped in the country, stands on the top of a ridge so high and steep that only real sportsmen can get there at all.

Norwegian Festivals

Christmas is a time for feasting and great merry-making throughout Norway. Preparations for this festival are made several weeks in advance: housewives stock their larders with piles of food and begin baking delicious cakes, pastries and puddings. A few days before Christmas, trees decorated with silver tinsel and foil, strings of lights and coloured balls, shimmer in the lighted windows of houses. Thick sprigs of evergreen, tied with ribbons, are nailed to front doors and hung inside houses. Little paper baskets are filled with nuts and raisins and hung on the lower branches of the Christmas trees; by tradition, these are not eaten until the 6th January.

On Christmas Eve most families go to church. The churches, too, are gaily decorated with evergreen and pale green winter mosses. After the trudge home through the deep-piled snow there follows the most important meal of the holiday. The Norwegians have always believed in eating well; this meal is certainly no exception. Boiled cod is the principal dish; it is covered with melted butter and eaten with a cucumber salad. To follow there is roast pork and *surkål*, which is thinly shredded cabbage soaked in salt water to make it taste slightly sour. To conclude the meal ice-cream or *riskrem*, a thick rice pudding mixed with whipped cream and topped with a fruit sauce, is served. Often a pudding made from boiled rice and milk is eaten instead of *riskrem*. This is called *risengrynsgrøt* and is served in small dishes. One of these dishes may contain a hidden almond. The person who finds it receives a small gift. This charming custom is similar to the hunt-the-coin in the British Christmas pudding.

After such a meal few people are capable of violent exercise. They all gather round the Christmas tree and sing the well-loved traditional carols. The head of the household or a friend of the family will dress up in the white whiskers and red robe of *Julenissen* (Father Christmas) and bring the children presents in a bulging sack which he carries over his shoulder. After the presents have been unwrapped there is more drinking and dancing, often continuing well into the small hours of the morning. The Norwegians are firm believers in not doing things by half measures.

In contrast, Christmas Day is much quieter. After church there follows a huge breakfast of cold pork, many varieties of cheeses and soused herrings. The children spend the rest of the day playing with their presents, singing carols or trying out new skis which are inevitable gifts in any Christmas stocking.

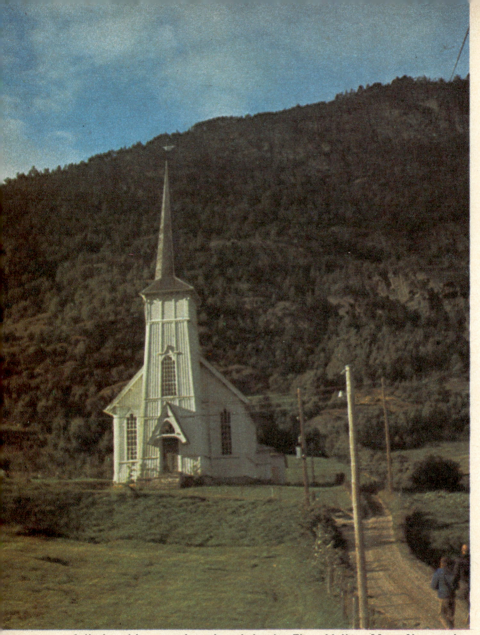

A little white wooden church in the Flam Valley. Most Norwegian churches, however small, have spires

The most popular festival in Norway is the Feast of St John, *Sankt Hans Aften,* or Midsummer Eve. The night of 23rd June is the shortest of the year. Entire families go to the seaside, a lake, or the nearest hill where bonfires are lit. Boats and cars everywhere are decorated with branches of birch leaves. Singing and dancing follow and there are often firework displays. Temporary stalls sell hot sausages, coffee and fruit drinks. Everyone stays to see the sun rise. The snow turns to silver and the branches of trees and slopes are diamond-spangled in the sudden bright light. The singing and dancing stop as everyone watches, a little breathlessly, a sight of quite unusual beauty. Shortly afterwards they go home to bed. Fortunately the following day, St John's Day, is a national holiday.

Constitution Day, which falls on 17th May, is a festival of great significance to all Norwegians. All schools, shops, factories and offices close and cities, towns and villages assume a festive air. In Oslo thousands of flag-waving school children, headed by brass bands, parade through the streets to the Royal Palace where the King takes the salute from the balcony. Thousands of small Norwegian flags flutter in honour of the royal family as they celebrate what must surely be Norway's bravest day.

To understand why Constitution Day is so important it is necessary to go back several hundred years to the time when Norway was hard-pressed by economic disaster. After the terrible menace of the Black Death in the fourteenth century a large part of the total population died. There were no longer sufficient people to work on the land and provide food for the remaining population. As a direct result, Norway was not strong enough to continue as a separate kingdom.

In 1319, Norway and Sweden were united under one king. Then, in 1397, the two countries were joined with Denmark, with Danish as the official language. Sweden left the union in 1523 but for centuries Norway had little history of her own until 1814, when the Danish power was broken. On 14th January, 1814, the Treaty of Kiel ceded Norway to Sweden.

Norway—Past, Present and Future

After hundreds of years of union with Denmark the flame of independence still burned in Norway. She refused to recognise the Treaty of Kiel and, on 17th May, 1814, representatives from all over the country signed Norway's first Constitution at Eidsvoll, near Oslo.

In spite of the fact that Norway now had a Constitution and

The Parliament Building— home of the Storting—in Oslo

a *Storting*, or Parliament, she was still not entirely independent. She was forced to accept unwilling union with Sweden. Although they had separate parliaments and laws, they shared things common to both countries: the King of Sweden was also the King of Norway.

Finally, in 1905, the Norwegian people were asked to make a choice. The result of this referendum was an overwhelming majority for complete independence for Norway. For her King Norway chose the Danish Prince Carl. During the following year, with his wife Princess Maud (youngest daughter of King Edward VII of Great Britain) as Queen, the Prince assumed the title of King Haakon VII and was crowned with great rejoicing in Oslo Cathedral.

The Royal Family are greatly loved in Norway. They live very close to their subjects, identifying themselves closely with the affairs of the country. The King, when he goes to open Parliament, drives in an ordinary car and wears everyday clothes, he does not wear royal robes and travel in a glittering coach. Noble titles were abolished in Norway by Act of Parliament over a hundred years ago. Because Norway is a constitutional monarchy the *Storting* is the supreme authority. The King may veto a Bill in the first instance; but if the Bill is subsequently passed by two successive *Stortings*, it becomes law without his assent. The *Storting* consists of 150 members, divided into an upper and a lower house. General Elections are held every four years. The Cabinet normally consists of twelve Ministers and a Prime Minister.

On 9th April, 1940, during the Second World War, Norway was occupied by the German armies. For the fiercely proud Norwegian people this was a shattering blow. In June of that year the King and his Government, to avoid arrest, sailed to Great Britain where they remained until the end of the war. The Germans set up a government under the Norwegian

The royal residence at Trondheim; an unpretentious home for a royal family which loves informality

The Royal Palace, Oslo

Vidkun Quisling—whose name came to be used in many countries to mean a traitor—but the people did all they could to oppose and upset the German plans.

Hundreds of brave Norwegians remained loyal to the King and endured dreadful hardships. Many died in concentration camps, either in Norway or in Germany. Others fled to the mountains where, with their intimate knowledge of the inhospitable countryside, they were able to harass the German troops. Fishing-boats sailed so often from Norway to the Shetland Isles, carrying refugees to safety, and returning with secret agents on board, that people talked of "taking the Shetland bus". In May, 1945, Norway was at last freed from German occupation and a new era of prosperity began. Then, after the total destruction of every town, village and building in Finnmark the Norwegians faced a stupendous building problem.

A guard outside the Royal Palace

Norway has now become much more outward-looking in her relations with other countries. After the war she gave up her former policy of neutrality and joined the defensive alliance called the North Atlantic Treaty Organisation (Nato). Her interest in other countries has made her an important ally of the Western European powers. The first Secretary General of the United Nations, Trygve Lie, was a Norwegian. Together with Sweden and Denmark she has helped establish a Scandinavian airline with services to many countries.

In trade and industry, too, Norway has made enormous strides in recent years. Apart from the few mines in the Spitzbergen islands, Norway has no coal. But nature has compensated for this lack in other ways. The great many lakes, rivers and waterfalls have been harnessed to provide the cheapest hydro-electric power in the world. It is so cheap that the Norwegian householder spends very little on electricity for cooking, lighting and heating.

This cheap electricity has other advantages too. It has led to the very rapid development of the metallurgical industry. Zinc, nickel and bauxite are imported into the country. Here it is refined and exported as finished metal. Iron ore is mined in several places and there are a number of iron and steel plants. Mo i Rana, in northern Norway, has the largest electric smelting furnaces.

The huge export of timber, ores and scrap iron calls for large carriers for long-distance haulage. These ships are becoming

The Norwegian flag flying from a small ship on a fjord. The Norwegians are very patriotic and loyal to their king and country

very much larger with the increase in foreign trade, but few are actually built in Norway. The orders are given to foreign shipyards.

Norway is also one of the first small countries to use atomic energy for peaceful purposes. There is a nuclear-powered paper mill at Halden in southern Norway. Radioactive isotopes, for use in industry and medicine, are exported to many countries throughout the world.

Unlike many countries where mass-production has taken over from the traditional skill of the craftsman the Norwegian worker takes pride in turning out fine work. This skill is reflected in glass, pottery, pewter ware, stainless steel cutlery,

toys and furniture. Norwegian products are particularly outstanding for their simplicity of design and construction. It is
not surprising, therefore, that there is a ready world market for
all types of Norwegian goods.

Norway is a young, hopeful and developing society whose
aims and aspirations are set very much on the future. Her
skills, determination to succeed and superb scenery have made
this small country one of the most respected and admired in
the world.

Index